"Extraordinarily well-informed."
        —*The San Francisco Bay Guardian*

"An interesting annotated guide."
        —*The Armchair Detective*

In two to three hours of leisurely walking you can see every place Dashiell Hammett is known to have lived in San Francisco and the majority of locales in his master mystery *The Maltese Falcon.* You'll also see several places where the Continental Op, a nameless short fat detective who was Hammett's longest-running character, shot it out with hard-boiled criminals.

Follow Sam Spade in his quest for the fabled Maltese Falcon. Follow Hammett himself as he works for the Pinkerton Detective Agency on the infamous Fatty Arbuckle case. See the spot where Miles Archer, Spade's partner, met swift death in the fog.

Discover a new San Francisco, the city as seen by its greatest mystery writer, with the DASHIELL HAMMETT TOUR.

"Those of us who have promised ourselves we would map out a walking tour of Hammett's San Francisco have been bested. It's been done! Not only done—but done well, with a loving attention to detail. Don Herron has put this tour together and it's a winner."
                        MYSTERY

also by Don Herron:

*Echoes from the Vaults of Yoh-Vombis;
A Compendium of the Life of George F. Haas*

forthcoming volumes in the
Literary Walks in San Francisco Series:

#2: Fritz Leiber Tour

#3: Telegraph Hill, Nob Hill, and Russian Hill

and others

DASHIELL HAMMETT TOUR ™

Don Herron

dawn heron press

ISBN 0-939790-02-5

Unless otherwise credited,
all photographs are by Mary Spoerer.
Calligraphy by Warren Thompson.

Manufactured in the United States of America.

DASHIELL

$6.95

order from:
Don Herron
537 Jones St. #9207
San Francisco, California 94102

For Brigid

dashiell hammett's
san francisco

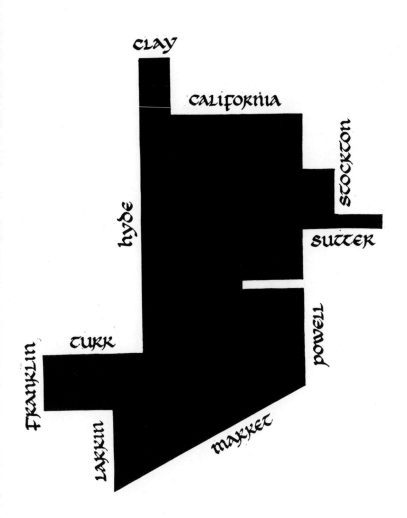

CLAY

CALIFORNIA

STOCKTON

hyde

SUTTER

TURK

POWELL

FRANKLIN

LARKIN

market

dashiell hammett

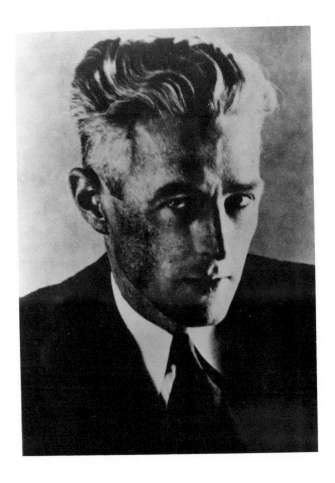

Dashiell Hammett, 1920s

Dashiell Hammett

Samuel Dashiell Hammett lived in San Francisco from 1921 to 1930. During those eight years he wrote most of his fiction, the now famous tales of hard-boiled private eyes such as *The Maltese Falcon* and *Red Harvest*. His characters Sam Spade—blond, slope-shouldered, Satan-faced—and the Continental Op—a nameless short fat detective—gumshoed grooves in foggy Frisco streets.

Born in St. Mary's County, Maryland, on May 27, 1894, Hammett was the son of Richard Thomas Hammett and Annie Bond Hammett. His middle name "Dashiell" derives from his mother's French family, De Chiel. He, a brother, and a younger sister were raised in the cities of Philadelphia and Baltimore.

When Hammett was fourteen, his father took sick. It was necessary for Hammett to quit Baltimore Polytechnic Institute, the high school he was attending, to get a job. Hammett never went back to high school and did not go to college.

From the family home at 212 North Stricker in Baltimore Hammett went out to a long series of short-lived jobs. Initially he worked for the Baltimore and Ohio Railroad. In time he served as a stevedore, messenger, common laborer, freight clerk, and nail machine operator in a box factory. These jobs bored him. Often he would not bother to show up for work on time, and the story is that he was often fired.

When Hammett was about twenty-two years old

he was looking for work once again, and saw an odd employment ad in the Baltimore daily paper. From the way the ad was worded, he could not tell exactly what sort of job it offered, but decided to give it a shot anyway. He went down to the Continental Building for an interview. The job: hire in as an operative for the Pinkerton Detective Agency.

Hammett hired in. Suddenly, he had a stimulating job, and assignments that required guts and intelligence! Working out of the Baltimore office, he trained under Assistant Superintendent James Wright, the man who, as Hammett told Ellery Queen many years later over luncheon in New York, would serve as the physical model for the Continental Op.

Once he was broken in, however, he got to work on cases all over the country. In Washington, D.C. during the early days of World War I, he shadowed a man suspected of being a secret agent for Germany; he later wrote that this man was the most boring subject he ever had to follow, but said too that he used him as the model for Caspar Gutman, the fat man in *The Maltese Falcon*. In Pasco, Washington, he arrested an oily little guy who had been forging checks; this fellow appeared as the perfumed rogue Joel Cairo in the Sam Spade novel. In Stockton, California, he arrested a hold-up man the newspapers called the Midget Bandit. The Midget Bandit stuck up a filling station in Stockton, then fled to Los Angeles. The owner of the station, when interviewed by the press, made some unwise remarks about the robber. For example, he described the Midget Bandit as "a runt" and went into detail about what he would do if the runt ever came back. These remarks were unwise, because apparently the Midget Bandit collected his press clippings. He bought the Stockton paper, read the article, said "By God, I'll show him," stole a car, and drove back to Stockton to rob the station again. Hammett caught him. When he wrote *The Maltese Falcon* years later, Hammett used the Midget Bandit as the model for Wilmer Cook, the young gunman, traveling with Caspar Gutman, who threatens to "fog" Sam Spade if he doesn't "lay off."

Hammett said he got his first promotion with Pinkerton by capturing a man who had stolen a ferris wheel. He also said that after he turned the crook in, the man escaped and took the ferris wheel with him, and was never found again. Obviously, this line of work was infinitely more interesting than operating a nail machine in a box factory.

One unpopular aspect of Pinkerton work in those days, however, was that the operatives often acted as strikebreakers against the unions which were forming in America. Hammett did some of that work, as a strikebreaker for the Anaconda Copper Company in Butte, Montana, against the Industrial Workers of the World. He later admitted that in those days "he was not politically aware," but apparently the seeds of his later communist political philosophy were sown then. An officer of Anaconda Copper offered Hammett $5,000 to assassinate labor organizer Frank Little. They figured a detective would pick up so much money gladly enough in exchange for a murder, but they figured wrong. Hammett turned their offer down. Later Frank Little and three other union men were lynched by a mob during the so-called Everett Massacre, a mob apparently spurred on by company forces.

In June, 1918, Hammett interrupted his work with Pinkerton to enlist in the Motor Ambulance Corps. He was stationed about thirty miles from Baltimore during his year of service. Two noteworthy events occurred while he was in the army. Once when driving an ambulance loaded with patients, Hammett hit an obstacle of some sort in the road, tipped the ambulance over, and spilled his passengers out into the roadway. Of course, the ambulances were pulled by mules in those days, yet the incident was traumatic for Hammett nonetheless. His wife recalled that he refused to drive a car after that incident; he was unlicensed to drive in California. Yet Lillian Hellman, the playwright Hammett lived with the last half of his life, mentions occasions when he drove a car—so apparently he *could* drive, but did not like to.

The serious event was that Hammett was one of hundreds of thousands of people who contracted Spanish influenza in the epidemic of 1918. This disease weakened Hammett's respiratory system and paved the way for tuberculosis. T.B. was to plague Hammett's health for over a decade, especially during his years in San Francisco.

By May, 1919 Hammett was out of the army, and soon went back into Pinkerton employ. He transferred to the Pinkerton office in Spokane, Washington, only to have his tuberculosis suddenly become active. In November he found himself a patient in a U.S. Public Health Service hospital in Tacoma, located on the Puyallup Road which ran between Tacoma and Seattle. The place had been an Indian School for the Puyallup tribe until converted into hospital use at the end of World War I. The patients, according to Hammett, were half "lungers," half victims of shell-shock.

At the Cushman Hospital Hammett met a pretty young nurse named Josephine Dolan. She later recalled that Hammett was quiet, well dressed, and would read to the other patients. They went out to restaurants in downtown Tacoma and to parks. Occasionally they took ferry boat rides. Hammett kept in touch with her by correspondence after he was moved to the old Army hospital in Camp Kearney, near San Diego, and Josephine Dolan was transferred to the Cheyenne Hospital in Helena, Montana.

Hammett left Camp Kearney around May, 1921, and went back to Spokane briefly. He spent another week or two in Seattle, then came to San Francisco to meet Josephine Dolan. They were married July 6, 1921, in St. Mary's Cathedral on Van Ness Avenue. Originally, as Hammett recalled, they were intending to spend a couple of months in San Francisco on a prolonged honeymoon, then return to Hammett's native Baltimore to set up housekeeping. Once he had a taste of life in San Francisco, however, Hammett realized it was a lot of fun—while Baltimore, on second thought, seemed very dull indeed.

Hammett decided to stay in San Francisco.

For eight years Hammett lived here. In San Francisco he became a published writer. Many of his stories are set in this city, including the novels *The Big Knockover, The Dain Curse,* and *The Maltese Falcon.* In fact, most of his fiction was written during his residence here; of his six completed novels, all except one were drafted in Hammett's apartments on Eddy, Hyde, Post, and Leavenworth. His longest running series of stories, concerning the casework of an unnamed operative for the Continental Detective Agency, is set in San Francisco. So, of course, are the adventures of Sam Spade. And Nick Charles, even though he is in New York when the thin man is murdered, is also a resident here. Hammett was a San Francisco writer.

In 1930, with *Red Harvest* and *The Dain Curse* out in hardcovers from Alfred Knopf, Hammett decided to go where the money for writers was being made. He took rooms at 133 East 38th Street in New York, and reviewed books for the *New York Evening Post*. He continued his review work after moving to Hollywood later in the year, where he lived at 1551½ North Bronson Avenue.

In Hollywood in 1930 he met Lillian Hellman, then the twenty-four year old wife of screenwriter Arthur Kober, later an internationally famous playwright. They began a relationship that would last thirty years, until Hammett's death in 1961.

Also in 1930 *The Maltese Falcon* appeared in hardcover from Knopf. Warner Brothers purchased the film option, paying Hammett $8500 for *all* movie rights to the novel. In 1931 "The Maltese Falcon," starring Ricardo Cortez as Sam Spade, appeared in theatres around the country; it bombed in the box office. In 1936 Warner Brothers tried again with a very loose remake called "Satan Met a Lady," starring Bette Davis, with Warren William as detective Ted Shayne and no black bird in sight; it too bombed. In 1941, John Huston directed Humphrey Bogart in the definitive film version, a tremendous box-office success. But Hammett got no money out of it. And the $8500 was long since spent.

It did not take long, however, for Hammett to wise up. Back in New York in 1933 with Lillian Hellman, he began work on his last detective novel, aimed at restocking a near empty bank account. Writing in cramped rooms in the Sutton Club Hotel, managed by his friend Nathaniel West, Hammett pulled together a formula that would knock over New York and Hollywood both with the urbane husband-and-wife sleuthing of Nick and Nora Charles. The Charles' dog Asta was named after a dog owned by the wife of Hammett's friend, humorist S. J. Perelman. Nora Charles was modeled on Lillian Hellman, and the novel was dedicated to her. *The Thin Man,* published in 1934 by Knopf, climbed the bestseller lists. It is still Hammett's bestselling novel. A film series followed, starring William Powell and Myrna Loy as Nick and Nora; it too was tremendously successful. You may be sure that Hammett got more than $8500 for the film rights.

The Thin Man appeared serially in *Redbook* in 1933. Hammett and Hellman used the magazine payment to cover a few weeks spent in Miami, and then the time in the spring and summer of 1934 spent in a fishing camp in the Florida Keys.

For King Features Syndicate Hammett created a daily comic strip about a tough government man known only as "Secret Agent X-9." The strip was drawn by Alex Raymond, today famous as the creator of the science fiction strip "Flash Gordon." Hammett wrote two long episodes which appeared in 1934 and 1935, and plotted a couple of further adventures which were finished by house writers for King Features.

Hammett and Lillian Hellman lived in an island cottage off South Norwalk, Connecticut, in 1937, where she worked on her play "The Little Foxes." By this time Hammett was no longer working seriously on prose fiction. An occasional assignment for film and, later, radio would be his major writing after 1935. He devoted part of his energy to Hellman's work. He brought to her attention the trial on which she based "The Children's Hour," gave her detailed criticism of "The Autumn Garden" and wrote a speech in the last act of that play.

Hammett had moved around a lot in the thirties:

in February of 1939 he and Hellman attended the opening of "The Little Foxes" in his native Baltimore; by late 1939 he was in New York City; in 1940 he was back in Hollywood. By the end of 1940, however, Hammett had settled down with Lillian Hellman on her 130 acre farm in Pleasantville, New York. A radio program of "The Adventures of the Thin Man" brought in royalties during 1941 and 1942. Hammett even served as president of the Writers League of America—until September, 1942, when he decided to once more join the army.

Hammett was then forty-eight years old. He did not have to join the army. Initially, he was refused induction because his teeth were too bad. He had his teeth pulled. They let him in. He was stationed in the Aleutian Islands on Adak and Kiska, a corporal in charge of the servicemen's newspaper. The young troops, by and large, had no idea he was a famous writer. They called him "Grandpop" or "Pop," borrowed money, asked his advice. Hammett enjoyed it. The army was one of his favorite institutions. He spent his last six months in Anchorage, Alaska, before leaving the service by September, 1945.

Back in the states, Hammett merchandised "The Adventures of Sam Spade" radio show in 1946, featuring Howard Duff as the voice of Sam Spade. Also in 1946 he created a character expressly for the airwaves, a sort of a continuation of his heavyset Continental Op and a nice counterpart to the Thin Man. The show began: "There he goes! Into that drug store. He's stepping on the scales. Weight: 237 pounds. Fortune: Danger! Who is he? The Fat Man . . . . " ("The Fat Man" probably had the most appropriate sponsor in the history of radio—

Pepto Bismol!) In 1948 "The New Adventures of the Thin Man" ran on NBC radio. Royalties were steady from these shows and from the paperback collections of Hammett's short fiction which Ellery Queen edited and saw into print, beginning with *The Adventures of Sam Spade, The Continental Op,* and *The Return of the Continental Op,* all published in 1945.

Hammett was an instructor in creative writing at the Jefferson School of Social Services in New York in 1947. He still spent most of his time in Pleasantville with Hellman, but soon he would be taken forcibly from that life, and Hellman would have to sell her farm.

Politically, Hammett leaned toward communism later in life. He agreed to have his name listed as a bail bond fund trustee of the Civil Rights Congress, although he never had reason to go to their offices. Four communists out on bail from that fund skipped out. The House Committee on Un-American Activities found this reason enough to subpoena Hammett and some other people connected with the bail bond fund, to ask for names of contributors. Hammett, an honorary trustee, did not know the names of contributors. He was angry because he felt he was being pushed around simply for holding his political convictions. When he appeared in court, he refused to give names. He refused to say he had no names to give. He was sentenced to six months in prison for contempt of court.

On July 10, 1951 he was put into the West Street Jail in New York City. Later he was transferred to a federal penitentiary in West Virginia and from there to a prison in Kentucky. He got a month off for good behavior and was freed December 11, 1951.

Two days after he entered jail the IRS froze all royalties from books, films, radio, alleging Hammett owed them back taxes. They hit him for $140,000, taken from the accumulated account, in 1956. At that time the only Hammett production was a television series of the Thin Man, from which Hammett received no royalties, having sold the dramatic rights earlier. The unfavorable publicity given to him as a "communist writer" scared commercial sponsors. His radio shows were off the air. The last Powell-Loy Thin Man film appeared in 1947, with a movie adapted from "The Fat Man" radio series in 1951 the last screen appearance of a Hammett character in his lifetime. Another collection of Hammett stories edited by Ellery Queen, *Woman in the Dark,* appeared in 1952; the next collection, *A Man Named Thin,* would not appear until 1962.

Hammett's last decade was bleak, not alone because of finances. His health was declining. The imprisonment, combined with his history of heavy smoking and drinking, his bouts with serious illness such as the tuberculosis, contributed to a physical breakdown. The last few years Hammett spent his life as a near invalid.

He would make a last try at fiction, however. In 1952 he rented a cottage in Katonah, New York, piled it up with his books and gadgets and unanswered mail, and sat down to write. "Tulip," a largely autobiographical mainstream novel, was the result. He never finished the book; the fragment he left was published in *The Big Knockover* in 1966, edited by Lillian Hellman.

In 1953 Hammett was called before the Senate Internal Security Subcommittee hearings conducted by Senator Joseph McCarthy, a televised spectacle during which McCarthy asked Hammett if he thought the United States should allow books by Communist writers in its overseas libraries for servicemen, when the government was spending millions every year to fight the spread of Communism. Hammett replied that if the government wanted to fight the spread of communism, in his opinion it should not allow any libraries at all.

Hammett, in increasingly poor health, gave up his cottage in 1957 and moved in with Lillian Hellman. From then until his death he lived at her New York City apartment at 63 East 82nd Street or her place on Martha's Vineyard.

Hammett died in Lenox Hill Hospital in New York City on January 10, 1961—cancer of the lungs was the major cause of death. He is buried in Arlington National Cemetery.

Dashiell Hammett's
San Francisco

James Flood Building, 1920s

Photo courtesy of San Francisco Archives, San Francisco Public Library

ÒASHIELL HAMMETT'S SAN FRANCISCO

Hammett came to San Francisco in June of 1921 to meet Josephine Dolan. They were married July 6, 1921 in St. Mary's Cathedral on Van Ness Avenue. When they decided to live in San Francisco, rather than return to Hammett's native Baltimore, Hammett once again hired in with the Pinkerton Detective Agency. He worked for them until early in 1922. Later that year he got a job writing advertising copy for Samuels Jewelers on Market Street by day. By night, he sat in his apartment and worked on his hard-boiled detective fiction—which is the reason you hold this guide book in your hands today.

The tour starts where Larkin crosses McAllister, at the:

1. San Francisco Public Library

This huge building of gray stone was a frequent stop for Hammett. His wife recalled, in particular, a period in which Hammett came here every day. In 1923 while working in the advertising department of Samuels Jewelers Hammett had bouts with hemorrhaging in his lungs. The tuberculosis was viciously active. On one occasion Hammett was found lying unconscious on the floor in a pool of blood he had coughed up. Naturally, he was sent home to rest. At that time he lived in Eddy Street. During his period of convalescence he would walk every afternoon the three blocks down Larkin to the library to read. Hammett was a prolific reader. After scanning the pulp magazines of the day, he figured he could do as well with a story. His first work had appeared in print by late 1922 in such pulps as *Brief Stories* and *Black Mask.*

map 1

1. SAN FRANCISCO PUBLIC LIBRARY
2. CIVIC CENTER PARK
3. CITY HALL
4. 580 McALLISTER
5. 408 TURK

From the library head west through:

2. Civic Center Park

Josephine Dolan held this block-square park to be her favorite in the city, probably because she lived close to it most of her time in San Francisco. In an interview in *City of San Francisco* magazine, Novem-

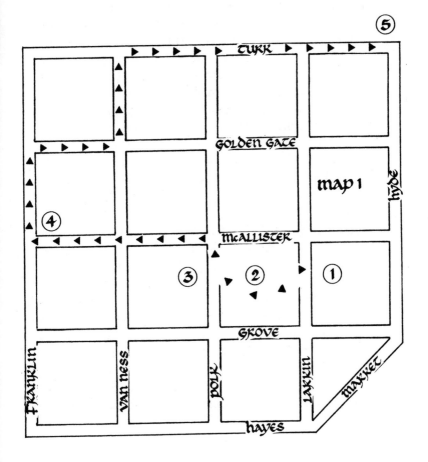

ber 1975, she said that she often would bring their first baby, Mary Jane, to the park in the afternoon, sit on the benches and talk with the other ladies, while Hammett would stay home in their Eddy Street apartment to cook supper. He liked to fix hamburger with lettuce. When they could afford it, he liked to have ground round. In the early 1920s they often could not afford ground round. It's said that Hammett made $105 a month as an operative for Pinkerton. The apartment in Eddy Street rented for $45 a month, leaving small margin for the purchase of ground round. Mrs. Hammett thought that Hammett's subsequent job as an advertising writer for Samuels Jewelers paid no better. And as a beginning writer for the pulp magazines, Hammett made little profit. On the average the pulps paid 1¢ a word for material. Two ways existed to make money as a pulp fictioneer: write millions of words a year or make a popular name for yourself so that your by-line heralded on a cover of *Black Mask* or *Detective Fiction Weekly* would sell thousands of copies of the issue—then perhaps the editors would consider shelling out the princely sum of 4¢, 5¢, maybe even 6¢ a word for your stories. Erle Stanley Gardner was one of those millions of words a year authors, writing hundreds of stories for the wood pulp publications, and later completing eighty-two novels about Perry Mason. Gardner, as A.A. Fair, also wrote twenty-nine novels about detectives Bertha Cool and Donald Lam. Hammett was never in that league. He wrote about one hundred pieces of short fiction and only six novel length works. It was not until 1926 that he was popular enough to command a higher word rate, allowing him to give up his job at Samuels and live from his writing, at which time he began to work on the novels which would take him to New York, Hollywood, and the big money.

The massive domed building directly across Civic Center Park from the library is:

3. City Hall

I like to look at City Hall as a symbol of the law in 1920s San Francisco, since the old Hall of Justice of Hammett's time long since has been torn down. That building stood on Kearney Street opposite Portsmouth Square (where the gigantic Holiday Inn stands today). If you've seen any hard-boiled detective movies or read any hard-boiled detective books, you know of course that the Hall of Justice is the place the hard-boiled dick goes to crackwise with the law. In *The Maltese Falcon* Sam Spade is called into the district attorney's office for questioning. The D.A. has with him an assistant district attorney and a male stenographer, who writes down every word said. The D.A. asks Spade to hazard a theory about the murders of Miles Archer, Spade's partner, and the criminal Floyd Thursby. Spade says: "My guess might be excellent, or it might be crummy, but Mrs. Spade didn't raise any children dippy enough to make guesses in front of a district attorney, an assistant district attorney, and a stenographer." Spade proceeds to tell off the D.A. Scribbling furiously, the stenographer tries to keep up with the rapid-fire dialogue. Spade asks him: "Getting this all right, son? Or am I going too fast for you?" The stenographer says he's getting it all right. Spade says good, tells the D.A. if he wants to see him again to call Sid Wise, his lawyer, and slap a subpoena on him. Then he stalks out. He probably slammed the door behind him, too.

Walk around the north side of City Hall on McAllister Street, cross at Van Ness Avenue, and go another block to the corner of McAllister and Franklin. The building on the northeast corner is:

4. 580 McAllister

In "The Whosis Kid," one of the series of twenty-eight short stories about the gumshoe work of the never-named Continental Op, the jewel thief Ines Almad has her apartment in this building—on a top

580 McAllister

floor in the rear, at the east end. According to Hammett, this story was a prototype for his famous Sam Spade novel. In a special introduction to the 1934 Modern Library reprint of *The Maltese Falcon* (the first detective novel to appear in a Modern Library edition—it eventually went through fifteen printings), Hammett wrote that the Spade novel came about because " . . . somewhere I had read of the peculiar rental agreement between Charles V and the Order of the Hospital of St. John of Jerusalem, that in a short story called 'The Whosis Kid' I failed to make the most of a situation I liked, that in another called 'The Gutting of Couffignal' I had been equally unfortunate with an equally promising denouement, and that I thought I might have better luck with these two failures if I combined them with the Maltese lease in a longer story."

(The lease required the gift of one living falcon *each year* to Emperor Charles from the Knights Hospitaliers, as *rent* for the entire island of Malta. Hammett, who had been paying $45 *a month* for furnished rooms in Eddy Street, obviously was impressed by this arrangement.)

In "The Gutting of Couffignal" the Op is doing a job on Couffignal, an (imaginary) island in San Pablo Bay north of San Francisco. The assignment is the second most boring chore a detective can be stuck with: the Op is guarding wedding presents. (The *most* boring job is a divorce case, but Continental, like the Pinkerton Agency on which it is modeled, does not handle divorces.) A gang of crooks assaults the island, blowing up the one bridge to the mainland. They also blow open the bank and jewelry store, gutting them of loot, as they slaughter people left and right. These crooks are so mean they even kill the butler and steal the wedding presents the Op has been guarding.

Meanwhile, the Op hustles his short fat body over the island, trying to figure out who is behind the attack. Tussling with a crook, he sprains an ankle. He limps around, and by the time the Coast Guard finally arrives, he knows who the crooks are; the entire gang, with the exception of one member, is rounded up without further gunplay or bloodshed.

The mastermind, however, is still at large. She's a beautiful evil Russian princess the Op intends to nab personally. To get to the house she's in, the Op has to take a crutch from a one-legged newsboy—his sprained ankle will no longer carry his weight. He confronts Princess Zhukovski, and in another tussle the crutch is knocked out of his reach. But the Op seats himself in a chair and covers her with his .38 special. She tries to bribe him. All the loot is in the basement—the two of them can become partners and get away with it yet! The Op says he's not interested. She says he can have whatever he asks for; coming from a beautiful evil Russian princess in a story written for a pulp magazine, the meaning is clear enough. The Op thinks nix on that—he doesn't know where these dames get their ideas, anyway.

The Princess figures she can escape with her own skin, at least, since the Op cannot get up to stop her, and surely he would not shoot a woman. She starts to leave. The Op's in a tough spot: he cannot run her down and he's never shot a woman before. He shouts for her to stop. She keeps going. He pumps a bullet into her leg and she drops, stares at him in shock. The Op shouts at her: "You ought to have known I'd do it! Didn't I steal a crutch from a cripple?"

A case, as in *The Maltese Falcon,* of the beautiful evil lady *not* getting away with her crime.

In "The Whosis Kid" all the action occurs in San Francisco, including a shoot-out on the north sidewalk of McAllister just east of Ines Almad's apartment building, car chases in the Haight and North Beach, and more. The origins of *The Maltese Falcon* are obvious in this story. Ines Almad, the dapper

Edouard Maurois, and the young homicidal killer known as the Whosis Kid were all partners in a jewel robbery in Boston, until Ines pulled double and triple crosses—she was supposed to meet them with the jewels in Chicago, but told Maurois she would meet him in New Orleans, and told the Kid she'd meet him in St. Louis. Instead, she ditched them both and came to San Francisco with the loot. They track her down and the Op gets stuck in the middle. If you recall the plot of *The Maltese Falcon,* Brigid O'Shaughnessy and Joel Cairo are supposed to steal the *jewel-covered* black bird for the fat man, but Brigid betrays both Cairo and Caspar Gutman and comes via Hong Kong to San Francisco; they track her here and find Sam Spade in their path. Also, at the end of "The Whosis Kid" we find the principal characters all gathered in Ines Almad's apartment, waiting for her to reveal where she has hidden the jewels. In *Falcon* we find Spade, Brigid, Gutman, Cairo, and the young homicidal maniac Wilmer Cook all waiting in Spade's rooms for his secretary to bring in the black bird.

There the similarities fade. Even though *The Maltese Falcon* is one of the most famous *hard-boiled* mysteries ever written, it actually has little violence occur before your eyes—the murders all occur "offstage;" you never see the blood splatter on the page. But the Continental Op stories weren't so restrained. In fact, they are hallmarks of pulp violence. An early Op story in *Black Mask* was titled "Bodies Piled Up." The Op novel *Red Harvest* has almost every character meet violent death before the last page—ice picks in the back, bombings, machine-gunnings, if it was violent an Op story had it. "The Whosis Kid" was no exception to the rule. When the jewels finally turn up, the guns start blazing in Ines Almad's apartment in 580 McAllister. The San Francisco coroner must have been busy for weeks afterward.

Walk up Franklin Street and turn right into Golden Gate Avenue. Go north on Van Ness, then east on Turk and walk three blocks to Hyde Street. Here on the northwest corner of the intersection, where the Metro Parking lot now does business, once stood:

5. 408 Turk

The only known Hammett address to have been razed (as of this writing), 408 Turk was where Hammett kept a first floor room for a period early in the twenties. At the same time he and his wife had their apartment in Eddy Street, which rented for $45 a month. In 1921 Hammett was still an operative for Pinkerton at a salary of $105 a month. It's hard to see how he could have afforded a separate place, especially for the purpose his oldest daughter recalls he kept it. Interviewed along with her mother in the November 1975 issue of *City of San Francisco,* Mary Jane Hammett said her father "kept his India ink" in his room at 408 Turk, adding, "he used to do a lot of sketches." Josephine Dolan said to her shortly before this account of India ink was mentioned, "You were little, you know." Today, with Hammett's legend growing larger each year, it's hard to credit a recollection of "sketches" against the scenarios imagination draws forth—of a place for all night poker games or a room in which an op for Pinkerton could meet underworld contacts without involving his family . . . .

The truth behind Hammett's keeping this second apartment is less exciting. Because of his tuberculosis, Hammett was advised by doctors to limit his contact with his infant daughter; Mary Jane Hammett was born October 15, 1921. He kept this room away from Eddy Street to avoid infecting her with T.B.

Return one block west on Turk to Larkin and walk north to the next street, Eddy. Turn left and walk about fifty feet. The yellow apartment building with white trim on the north side of the street is:

6. 620 Eddy

Of Hammett's eight years in San Francisco, he spent five of them here in the Crawford Apartments, his main residence in the city. He and his wife set up house-keeping here in 1921 in a $45 a month furnished apartment. It had a living room, a small bedroom with a Murphy bed folding down out of the wall, a kitchen, and a bath. It was steam heated.

The Hammetts lived in 620 Eddy until 1925, when Hammett sent his wife and daughter to live with Josephine Dolan's relatives in Montana for six months. When they returned to the city, the Hammetts reunited in 620 Eddy, but in a larger apartment in this building. On May 24, 1926, a second daughter was born, named Josephine after her mother. By 1927

620 Eddy, the middle building

Hammett again sent his family away briefly; when they returned the same year they moved into 1309 Hyde Street.

Hammett suffered from hemorrhaging while in this building. During the attacks he would line up chairs leading to the bathroom, so he could support himself across the room by leaning on the chair backs. He finally was pronounced cured of tuberculosis in 1925.

Hammett began serious writing here in Eddy Street, working in the advertising department of Sam-

map 2

6. 620 eddy
7. 601 eddis
8. blanco's
9. 811 geary
10. 891 post

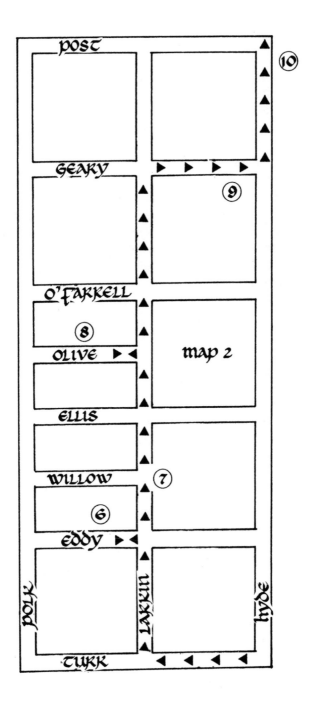

post

⑩

GEARY

⑨

O'FARRELL

⑧

OLIVE

map 2

ELLIS

WILLOW

⑦

⑥

EDDY

POLK

LARKIN

HYDE

TURK

uels Jewelers by day, by night going home and putting the Continental Op through the meatgrinder in story after story. In the 1926 city directory Hammett listed himself at this address as "advertising manager for A. S. Samuels Co." Yet that same year he quit his job at Samuels to devote his full energies to his fiction. He wrote directly at the typewriter, according to his wife. At their first apartment in Eddy Street he worked in the kitchen; when they moved into larger quarters in 1925 he wrote in the living room.

In the interview in *City* Mrs. Hammett distinctly recalled that their landlady here in the '20s was a bootlegger. She said, "We used to peek down out the window and see all the cops coming and going."

Return to Larkin and walk north half a block. Pause where Willow Alley enters Larkin and contemplate one of the most mysterious Hammett sites:

7. 601 Eddis

Eddis? The next street up is Ellis, the one recently left is Eddy, but where is *Eddis?* Ah, that's the question! In some stories, such as "The Whosis Kid," Hammett used identifiable streets and buildings. In other stories he was vague, as in "The House in Turk

Street"—wherein we know the Op is trapped in a single family house in a residential block of Turk, but no cross-street is ever mentioned. But in the story "Fly Paper" Hammett mated Eddy and Ellis and caused some new wrinkles to appear in the foreheads of his fans.

In the November 1975 issue of *City* Joe Gores had an article entitled "A Foggy Night," in which he tried to pinpoint all the buildings used in *The Maltese Falcon,* and as many sites from Hammett's Op stories as possible. Gores is the author of several detective novels, including the contemporary series about Daniel Kearney and Associates of San Francisco. Like Hammett, Gores was an investigator before turning to writing, working a dozen years as an eye, nine of them with the David Kikkert and Associates agency (which is to the Kearney series what Pinkerton is to the Continental Detective Agency). Gores says he became a detective out of his fascination with Hammett's Continental Op. Of course, his main connection to Hammett today is his 1975 novel, simply titled *Hammett.* It features Hammett in San Francisco in 1928, once more putting on gumshoes to solve the murder of a friend. Recently the novel was filmed with Francis Coppola as producer, Wim Wenders as director, and Frederic Forrest starring as Dashiell Hammett.

Gores in his article concludes that 601 Ellis was the address Hammett had in mind for 601 Eddis, since there never has been a 601 Eddy. But the story clearly says the apartment building overlooked Larkin Street. The 700 block of Ellis *begins* at Larkin; 601

Ellis looks out on Hyde Street. The 600 block of Eddy, however, *does* begin at Larkin.

Whichever street Hammett may have intended, "Fly Paper" ranks among his toughest scenarios. A woman is murdered using arsenic taken from fly paper. A man the Op is interviewing about the crime at 601 Eddis is gunned down before his eyes. The killer, a huge grifter name of Babe McCloor, leads the Op on a chase through the train yards and warehouse district. At the end of the pursuit the Op corners him in a dead end alley. McCloor's gun is out of ammunition, but he is confident he can tear the Op's head off and still escape—a few .38 slugs won't stop him! The short fat detective says the slugs will stop him if they smash his kneecaps. McCloor decides to try anyway and makes a rush. The Op shoots off one of the bruiser's kneecaps. McCloor lurches closer. The Op shoots the other. McCloor sinks to the ground. He clenches his teeth, says, "I didn't think you had sense enough to do it."

Continue north on Larkin, across Ellis, until Olive Street opens at midblock on the west side of the street. Turn into Olive and go down the alley. On the north side of Olive, slightly more than halfway through the block, stands the rear wall of a red brick building, easily spotted because of a huge vent pipe. Near the top of the wall, still discernable, is lettering for:

8. Blanco's

Blanco's was a restaurant where the Op ate a meal in the last Continental Op novel, *The Dain Curse.* (Go around to the front of the building today and you'll discover it houses The Great American Music Hall.) Hammett dedicated *The Dain Curse* to Albert S. Samuels, his employer at Samuels Jewelers, and placed about half the action in San Francisco—including the Op's run-in with a weird religious cult.

Blanco's in Olive Street

Return to Larkin, turn left and continue up the street to Geary. Turn right on Geary, walking on the south sidewalk toward downtown. Before you come to Hyde Street, stop in front of:

9. 811 Geary

This six story apartment building is where the respected science fiction, fantasy, and supernatural horror writer Fritz Leiber lived for several years, from late 1969, shortly after coming to San Francisco, until 1977 when he moved farther down Geary. It was here in 1974-75 that he wrote his supernatural horror novel *Our Lady of Darkness*. The hero of that book, Franz Westen, also "lives" at 811 Geary, in circumstances similar to Leiber's at the time. *Our Lady of Darkness* is a particularly fine San Francisco novel, but is of interest here mainly because Dashiell Hammett features as an actor in the narrative. (Finding Hammett used as a character in a novel of ghosts and horrors may startle some people; yet remember that the only story collection Hammett ever edited was *Creeps by Night* from the John Day Company in 1931, which featured supernatural tales by William Faulkner, John Collier, and other then well-known authors, as well as offering one of the earliest hardcover publications for tales by the *now* famous supernaturalists H.P. Lovecraft and Donald Wandrei.)

At Hyde, go north one block to Post Street. The four-story brick building on the southeast corner of the intersection is:

10. 891 Post

After separating from his wife late in 1927, Hammett moved into the Charing Cross Apartments, 891 Post Street. He lived here throughout 1928, but moved again in March, 1929. Freed from family responsibilities, Hammett sat down to write book-length fiction: he completed a final draft of *Red Harvest,* finished the serial version of *The Dain Curse* to appear in four issues of *Black Mask,* and started his next novel. In this new book he decided to get away from the Continental Op, who had just slugged and shot his way through *The Big Knockover, Red Harvest,* and *The Dain Curse.* Hammett created a new detective. His name was Sam Spade.

The Continental Op, as Hammett told Ellery Queen, was modeled on Pinkerton operative James Wright. But of his new detective Hammett said: "Spade had no original. He is a dream man in the sense that he is what most of the private detectives I worked with would like to have been and what quite a few of them in their cockier moments thought they approached. For your private detective does not—or did not ten years ago when he was my colleague—want to be an erudite solver of riddles in the Sherlock Holmes manner; he wants to be a hard and shifty fellow, able to take care of himself in any situation, able to get the best of anybody he comes in contact with, whether criminal, innocent by-stander or client."

The novel which Hammett had in first draft was *The Maltese Falcon,* perhaps his most famous book and certainly the most famous mystery set in San Francisco. Sam Spade in hat and trenchcoat, walking through the fog, is as firm a part of San Francisco's lore as the 1906 earthquake and fire is of her history. No other detective novel has excited so much interest here or sent so many people scurrying over the hills, as they shadow Sam Spade's movements in his search for the black bird.

Fritz Leiber wrote the first article which listed locales used in *The Maltese Falcon;* it was entitled "Stalking Sam Spade," and appeared in *California Living* for January 13, 1974. In that article Leiber concluded that Spade lived in an apartment building at Geary and Hyde, because Spade rides the Geary streetcar from downtown, debarks at Hyde, and goes "up" to his rooms—"up" stairs or an elevator, thought Leiber. But Joe Gores in "A Foggy Night," published the following year, points out a clue Leiber missed. At one point in *The Maltese Falcon* Spade goes out to see if Wilmer Cook, Gutman's boy gunman, is still watching his apartment. The line reads: "Post Street was empty when Spade issued into it." Obviously, then, Spade lives on Post, and came *up* Hyde from Geary after leaving the streetcar. And as

Gores points out, what is more natural than that Hammett would place Spade's apartment in the same building he himself lived in, at 891 Post?

From other clues in the novel I figure Spade's apartment was on the top floor overlooking Post Street. (Hammett stayed in 401.) When Spade issues into Post, he goes east a block (to Leavenworth),

891 Post; Hammett lived in #401, top floor, left corner window

crosses and walks west two blocks (to Larkin), then returns to his building (at Hyde). He does not turn down into Hyde to check for Wilmer Cook there, because anyone staking out 891 Post would be on Post Street where he could see the front door, the only entrance to the building. Since Spade from his window notices Wilmer loitering in doorways a couple of times, Spade's apartment must have overlooked Post.

We can be sure it's on the top floor because of the incident toward the end of the novel, when Gutman offers Spade $10,000 for the falcon—ten $1000 bills in an envelope. Spade hands the envelope to Brigid to hold, then gives it back to Gutman at his request; Gutman palms a bill and reports it missing. Spade makes Brigid go into the bathroom and remove her clothes, but before he searches her he says to Gutman and Joel Cairo: "The door will be open and I'll be facing it. Unless you want a three-story drop there's no way out of here except past the bathroom door." A three-story drop places Spade's apartment on the fourth and final floor.

It was in this apartment that Spade, at the end of *The Maltese Falcon,* set the edges of his teeth together and said to Brigid O'Shaughnessy: "I won't play the sap for you."

Continue up Hyde, north for six blocks—a long stretch which will impress upon you how the Op's feet must have felt after he shadowed some hard-boiled yegg from the bail bondsman's on Kearney to an eastbound ferry. Just across Clay Street on the west side you'll come to:

11. 1309 Hyde

The Locarno Apartments, where Hammett and his family moved in 1927, witnessed the break-up of his marriage late that same year. From 620 Eddy Street Hammett had sent his wife and daughters Mary Jane and Josephine to San Anselmo for a while; when they returned to San Francisco, they reunited in this apartment overlooking the cable car line. From here Hammett moved to 891 Post (Sam Spade's apartment) and Mrs. Hammett took the two girls, relocating in southern California. She filed for divorce in 1937. Hammett often saw his family during his years in Hollywood in the 1930s and 1940s, and spent the summer with them as late as 1950, when he was brought from New York to Hollywood by director William Wyler to write the screenplay for "Detective Story" (Paramont, 1951), starring Kirk Douglas—an assignment Hammett withdrew from after a couple of weeks. After 1951, his health began to fail, so that he could no longer make the trip from New York or

map 3

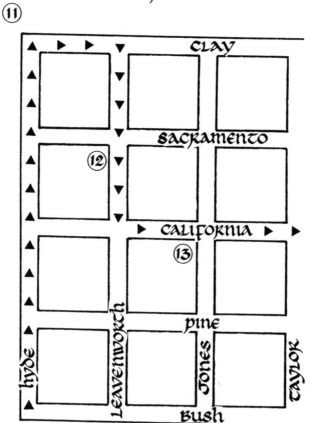

CLAY

SACRAMENTO

CALIFORNIA

PINE

BUSH

hyde

LEAVENWORTH

JONES

TAYLOR

map 3

11. 1309 hyde
12. 1155 LEAVENWORTH

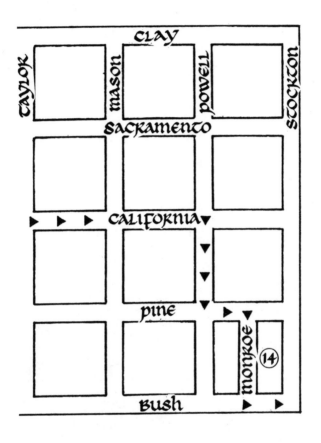

13. 1201 CALIFORNIA
14. 20 MONROE

55

Martha's Vineyard, where he was living with Lillian Hellman, to the West Coast to see his family. Upon his death January 10, 1961, Hammett left three-fourths of his estate to his daughters and one-fourth to Lillian Hellman.

1309 Hyde

1155 Leavenworth

*Return to Clay and head east uphill to Leaven-
worth, then right one block to the intersection of
Leavenworth and Sacramento. The building on the
southwest corner is:*

12. 1155 Leavenworth

The San Loretto Apartments were Hammett's final
address in San Francisco. He moved here early in

1929 from 891 Post Street and left here for New York later that year. For the first time he listed himself in the city directory as a "writer"; with both *Red Harvest* and *The Dain Curse* out in hardcover from Knopf in 1929, no one could argue the point.

Tradition in this building places Hammett's quarters in #2, a studio bedroom with a small kitchen and bath. In those days a Murphy bed folded from the wall, but it is gone now; the kitchen too is modernized. The first floor windows look out over Leavenworth at the south end of the building. If the tradition handed down from manager to manager is accurate, then #2 is the apartment in which Hammett completed the final draft of *The Maltese Falcon.*

Continue down Leavenworth to California, turn left and walk one block uphill to Jones Street. The tall building on the southwest corner is:

13. 1201 California

If you stand directly before the main entrance to the Cathedral Apartments, you'll see a green awning with a "C" in white emblazoned on it. Joe Gores in his essay "A Foggy Night" suggests that you look at that "C", but instead of thinking "Cathedral," think of the Coronet, the apartment building on California where Brigid O'Shaughnessy stays through most of *The Maltese Falcon*. Though not a definitive choice for the Coronet, it serves well. Spade, of course, is summoned to the Coronet by his client Miss Wonderly shortly after the murders of his partner Miles Archer and the gunman Floyd Thursby. She explains that her name really isn't Miss Wonderly but Brigid O'Shaughnessy, that she does not have a younger sister who is in trouble, but she's in trouble herself. She then says: "Help me. I've no right to ask you to help me blindly, but I do ask you. Be generous, Mr. Spade. You can help me. Help me." And Spade replies: "You won't need much of anybody's help. You're good. You're very good."

From the Cathedral Apartments at Jones Street continue along California toward downtown, passing the old James Flood mansion, the Fairmont, the Mark Hopkins. When you reach Powell, turn right and begin your descent from Nob Hill. Turn left into Pine, the first cross-street, and walk half a block on the south sidewalk. Turn right, down into Monroe Street, and you will come to:

20 Monroe

14. 20 Monroe

Hammett lived here briefly in 1926 during a separation from his family. Later they moved into 1309 Hyde. Hammett, after staying with them in that apartment for only a few weeks, relocated at 891 Post Street—where he would place Sam Spade's apartment in *The Maltese Falcon.* This place is largely of interest because of its tantalizingly close proximity to what is today the most famous Hammett site in San Francisco.

Follow Monroe down and turn left into Bush Street. Walk until you reach Stockton—only half a block, then cross Bush to where the two flights of stairs emerge at the top of the:

map 4

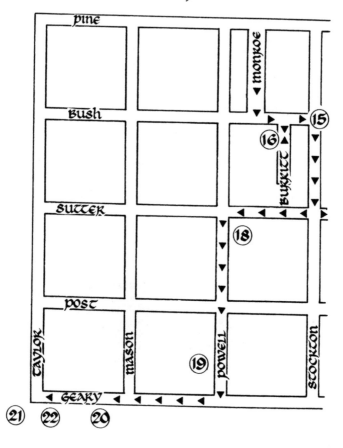

15. STOCKTON TUNNEL OVERPASS
16. BURRITT STREET
17. 111 SUTTER
18. SIR FRANCIS DRAKE

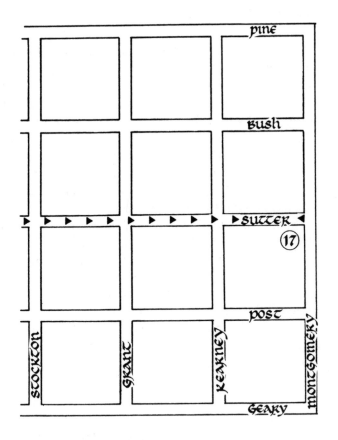

19. ST. FRANCIS
20. GEARY THEATRE
21. BELLEVUE HOTEL
22. CLIFT HOTEL

MAP 4

15. Stockton Tunnel

At 2 a.m. the telephone awakened Sam Spade in his apartment at 891 Post. He said, "Hello . . . . Yes, speaking . . . . Dead? . . . Yes . . . . Fifteen minutes. Thanks." He dressed, phoned for a taxicab, and had it drop him "where Bush Street roofed Stockton before slipping downhill to Chinatown." Then, "Spade crossed the sidewalk between iron-railed hatchways that opened above bare ugly stairs, went to the parapet, and, resting his hands on the damp coping, looked down into Stockton Street."

Spade looked down toward a vacant lot on the righthand side of Stockton, where the tall white Mc-Alpin apartment building stands today. A billboard fenced the lot from the sidewalk; three men were looking around the billboard. Flashlight beams flickered on the wall of the next building.

Spade left the parapet and walked through the night-fog a short distance west on Bush to where a small group of men stood looking into:

16. Burritt Street

Beneath the street sign a bronze plaque tells all, summing up in one sentence why this alley is the most sought after Hammett landmark in San Francisco: "On approximately this spot Miles Archer, partner of Sam Spade, was done in by Brigid O'-Shaughnessy." The first murder in *The Maltese Falcon!* The crime that led to other deaths, and put Sam Spade on the trail of the fabulous figurine of a black bird . . . . A *classic* site for any hard-boiled literary hiker.

Attempts to put up a plaque had been strangled by red tape, until in the late 1960s the famous San Francisco advertising man Howard Gossage combined forces with Warren Hinckle, journalist, founder of *Ramparts* magazine. They worded the plaque, ordered it—but before it could be installed, Gossage died. The plaque lay about Hinckle's house for five years, until one night in 1973 an anonymous literary historian spray painted "Miles Archer Was Shot Here" on the sidewalk in front of the Bush Gardens Restaurant, located in the Hotel Victoria on the northeast corner of Bush and Stockton Streets. This daring commando action drew much publicity to the need for a plaque. Hinckle brought it out, and it finally was installed on the side of the Matabelle Apartments in Burritt alley Tuesday, February 12, 1974 by James Kennedy, the owner of the building, by Marino Nibbi, a contractor, and by Supervisor Quentin Kopp.

Today the street sign reads "Burritt" in black letters on white, but Sam Spade came up to "a uniformed policeman chewing gum under an enameled sign that said *Burritt St.* in white against dark blue."

He walked halfway down the alley to meet Tom Polhaus of the homicide squad. On the left, where the white apartment building is today, a board fence ran along the alley. Past it "dark ground fell away steeply to the billboard on Stockton Street below."

Fifteen feet down the hill Miles Archer's corpse lay, lodged between a boulder and the slope of fog-damp earth.

When you leave Burritt alley, return to the Stockton Tunnel and descend the nearer flight of steps. Turn right at the bottom and walk a block down to Sutter Street. Standing on the corner, look left on Sutter and you will see a tall square modern skyscraper (the Wells Fargo Building, if anyone cares) dominating the skyline at the foot of Sutter Street. In front of this colossus is another tall structure, much older, ornate, with a green railing on the top. It is:

17. 111 Sutter

The Hunter-Dulin Building is the place Joe Gores in "A Foggy Night" pinpoints as the office building of Samuel Spade and Miles Archer. It is larger, more grand than one would expect of the building housing Spade's desk and file cabinets. But Gores' argument in its favor is painstaking and it matches the street directions given in *The Maltese Falcon* perfectly. I'm all for it, even though others have argued that Spade worked out of the old Hallidie Building at 130 Sutter. (Also, Sid Wise of Wise, Merican & Wise, Spade's lawyer, had his office in room 827 of a corner building at Sutter and Kearney, a block up Sutter from Spade.)

111 Sutter

You may choose to go the three blocks down Sut-
ter for a closer look at the Hunter-Dulin Building or
press on to the next site, going right on Sutter for one
block to Powell Street. On the southeast corner of
the intersection stands the:

18. Sir Francis Drake Hotel

In "A Foggy Night" Gores tries to locate every
building mentioned in *The Maltese Falcon.* In the
case of Spade's apartment in 891 Post Street at Hyde
and Spade's office in 111 Sutter, I think he chose the
definitive sites. Yet in other instances, to complete
his thesis, he grabbed for specific sites where the descriptions are too vague to allow an accurate deduc-
tion. The most obvious example of this process occurs when he selects a first *and* a second choice for
the original of the Alexandria, the hotel where Caspar Gutman stays.

Gores' first choice for the Alexandria is the Sir
Francis Drake, based upon the scene where Wilmer
Cook, the fat man's gunsel, meets Spade outside the
detective's office building. Cook has a gun in both
pockets of his overcoat. He tells Spade Gutman wants
to see him. It is only a short walk up Sutter to the
Alexandria—four blocks from 111 Sutter to the Sir
Francis Drake. They take the elevator to the twelfth
floor. As they go down the hallway Spade tackles
Wilmer and takes his guns. When they enter Gutman's
suite Spade says: "A crippled newsie took them away
from him, but I made him give them back." (A line

indicating the novel's origins in the Op story "The Gutting of Couffignal", which had Hammett's best crippled newsboy.)

But when Spade first went into Gutman's suite earlier in the book, it said: "Doors in three of the room's walls were shut. The fourth wall, behind Spade, was pierced by two windows looking out over Geary Street." The Sir Francis Drake is two blocks away from Geary and is not the definitive Alexandria.

Go downhill on Powell Street one block to Post. On your left you'll see Union Square, one of San Francisco's most famous square blocks. Directly across Powell Street from the park looms the twelve-story stone structure known worldwide as the:

19. St. Francis Hotel

In *The Maltese Falcon* Miles Archer shadows Brigid O'Shaughnessy and Floyd Thursby from the lobby of the St. Mark Hotel to his death in Burritt alley. The *original* of the St. Mark would be, because of the similar name, either the St. Francis here or the Mark Hopkins on Nob Hill. In the novel the St. Mark is described as a first class hotel, which both these businesses are, but also as an established hotel with a firm tradition and reputation in the city. In 1928

St. Francis Hotel, 1920s

Photo courtesy of San Francisco Archives, San Francisco Public Library

when Hammett started writing the Sam Spade novel, the St. Francis was considered San Francisco's number one hotel, closely followed by the Palace on Market Street. The Mark Hopkins had opened for business in December 1926, slightly more than a year before, and had not yet established landmark fame. So when you enter the main doors of the St. Francis on Powell and go into the red carpeted lobby (in the 1920s a circular registration desk ushered in the guests, but check-in services today are in the St. Francis Tower addition, past the original lobby), you're in the vast room where Miles Archer began work on his last case.

The most famous case Hammett worked on as a Pinkerton operative in San Francisco originated here in the St. Francis, when the famous Hollywood silent comedian Roscoe "Fatty" Arbuckle had a party on Monday, September 5, 1921 in a suite of three rooms —1219, 1220, and 1221, overlooking the corner of Powell and Geary Streets. After the party Arbuckle was accused of raping the young actress Virginia Rappe; Rappe died September 9th, and Arbuckle found himself on trial for murder in one of the most sensational cases ever to rock Hollywood and America. Hammett worked for Arbuckle's defense lawyers gathering evidence. It was Hammett's opinion that Arbuckle was framed "by some of the corrupt local newspaper boys." After two hung juries, the third panel completely acquited Arbuckle of any wrongdoing, but the scandal had ruined his career by that time. Today Arbuckle's name carries the taint of the scandal rather than the vindication of the acquital, and his films rarely are shown. Before the trial he was second only to Charlie Chaplin as the favorite film comedian in the world.

When you leave the lobby of the St. Francis turn right toward Geary Street. Another right into Geary will point you westward. Walk one block to Mason. Just beyond Mason, on the south side of the street, you'll see the ornate facade of the:

20. Geary Theatre

This theatre at 450 Geary is where the perfumed rogue Joel Cairo had tickets to a play in *The Maltese Falcon.* Since Cairo and Spade at one point pause outside the theatre in front of a poster of George Arliss costumed as Shylock, the play must have been *The Merchant of Venice* with its appropriate "pound of flesh" scene (certainly Spade handed more than a pound to the law at the end of the novel).

Continue west on Geary to the next street, Taylor. The building on the southwest corner is the:

21. Bellevue Hotel

The Bellevue, because of the similar name, is accepted as the model for the Belvedere, the hotel in which Joel Cairo stays in *The Maltese Falcon.* When the novel was serialized in four parts in *Black Mask,* Spade asked Luke, the Belvedere house dick, about Cairo. Luke replied, "Oh, *her!"*

Still at the intersection of Geary and Taylor, the building on the southeast corner is the:

22. Clift Hotel

This building is Gores' second choice for the original of the Alexandria, Caspar Gutman's hotel. It does have windows looking out directly over Geary Street, but by no stretch of logic is it a short walk *up Sutter* from the Hunter-Dulin Building. I think one of two situations is occurring here: 1) Hammett did not have a specific hotel in mind for the Alexandria, hence the contradictions regarding Sutter and

Geary Streets, or 2) Hammett *did* intend for a hotel on Sutter such as the Sir Francis Drake to be the model for his descriptions of the Alexandria, but in writing "the fourth wall . . . was pierced by two windows looking out over *Sutter* Street" he wrote *Geary* by accident and it got into print. Whatever the explanation may be, a definitive model for the Alexandria seems impossible to locate.

An interesting idiosyncracy of *The Maltese Falcon* is that every hotel a character lives in in the novel is under a faked name, but every place Sam Spade *eats* in the book is an actual restaurant under its real name. One wonders how many free meals Hammett may have received in exchange for immortalizing States Hof Brau, Tait's, John's Grill . . . .

Return east on Geary to Powell, turn right and walk down two blocks to the intersection with Ellis Street. The building on the northwest corner is:

23. 120 Ellis

This place, the old Woodstock Rooms, is where Hammett stayed immediately before he and Josephine Dolan were married July 6, 1921.

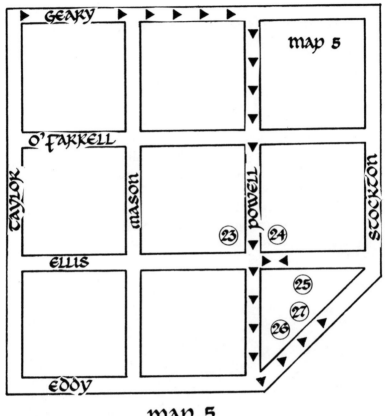

map 5

23. 120 ELLIS
24. 114 POWELL
25. JOHN'S GRILL
26. JAMES FLOOD BUILDING
27. SAMUELS JEWELERS

Directly across Powell on the northeast corner is:

24. 114 Powell

Now the Hotel Union Square, in 1921 it was named the Golden West Hotel. This building is where Josephine Dolan stayed before the marriage. The ceremony took place in the old St. Mary's Cathedral at 1155 Van Ness. (This historic cathedral was razed by fire some years ago. A new cathedral, resembling the inside of a washing machine, carries on the name at Geary and Gough Streets.)

120 Ellis, left front, and 114 Powell, right

From the intersection of Ellis and Powell you should be able to spot the next site at 63 Ellis Street:

25. John's Grill

John's Grill is one of two restaurants where Sam Spade ate in *The Maltese Falcon* which have survived the decades since Miles Archer's death. The other is the Garden Court of the Palace Hotel (now the Sheraton-Palace, at Market and New Montgomery).

But John's is the one to recognize its historic role, and take appropriate action. At 7 p.m. on January 16, 1976, they officially opened upstairs a special Dashiell Hammett Room (the upstairs room, by the way, was added to John's in 1921, the year Hammett moved to San Francisco). It features photographs of Hammett and authors who have written about him, such as Fritz Leiber, Joe Gores, William F. Nolan; as well as photos of detectives such as David Fechheimer and Hal Lipset. Around the walls are still photos with dialogue captions from the definitive film version of "The Maltese Falcon," starring Humphrey Bogart as Sam Spade; you walk around the room and the movie seems to unroll before your eyes. A glass case contains a selection of books by Hammett, books about Hammett, Lauren Bacall Bogart's autograph, even a facsimile of the fabled Black Bird itself.

John's menu offers three items with the Hammett fan in mind. First, the cover of the menu may be purchased; it features an art deco painting of Hammett standing before the grill's door. John's serves a special drink, the Bloody Brigid (named by the California Historical Society), in a souvenir glass. And they offer a "Sam Spade's Chops" dinner—rack of lamb, baked potato and sliced tomatoes. (In the novel, incidentally, Spade orders "chops, baked potato, and sliced tomatoes"—the animal the chops comes from is not mentioned.)

Today John's Grill is a major attraction for hungry Hammett fans—for most people the next place to go after a trip to Burritt alley.

Next to John's is a cavernous entrance at 71 Ellis Street, which you should enter if it is open for public passage when you gumshoe your way through this tour; if it's not, walk around the building, past Woolworth's and the Powell Street cable car turntable, to the cavernous front entrance at:

26. 870 Market

The James Flood Building is where Hammett worked as an operative out of suite 314, Pinkerton's San Francisco office, under Resident Superintendent Philip Geauque. Hammett had been about twenty-two years old when he started with Pinkerton. He was twenty-seven when he signed in with the local office in 1921, and would resign from the agency permanently before his next birthday on May 27, 1922. Over a five year period he was on active assignment for slightly less than three years.

The casework in San Francisco was varied. He sleuthed around for Fatty Arbuckle's lawyers. He dismissed a housekeeper for a woman who came into the office and said she could not do it herself. Once he was a shadow on a man walking up Stockton Street, but was unaware the man had a partner. The partner coshed Hammett on the head with a brick. The rest of his life Hammett had a dent in his skull shaped like the corner of a brick, in addition to scars on his legs

Entrance to James Flood Building

from earlier scraps with grifters. He was paid $105 a month salary and was on call twenty-four hours a day, every day. If crime was afoot, the operatives would be hard at its heels. If not, they would be idle, waiting for the next assignment.

Hammett quit the Pinkerton Agency early in 1922. His health was no longer stable enough to permit him to continue as a gumshoe—indeed, until he finally was pronounced cured of tuberculosis in 1925, Hammett felt that he lived on borrowed time. Also, he was by then becoming more interested in writing, even as detective work was losing its fascination. A more definite reason for resigning came about in this way: the Oceanic liner *Sonoma* on a run from Sydney, Australia to San Francisco had stolen from its strongbox $125,000 in gold specie. Pinkerton was brought in on the case and all but $20,000 was recovered, the major part of it hidden in shipboard fire hydrants or strapped in oil cans floating near the liner in San Francisco Bay. The *Sonoma* was readying for departure. Superintendent Geauque told Hammett he would have to go on the ship back to Australia and try to recover the last of the specie *en route*. Hammett thought this plan was great—a free trip to Australia! But the Pinkertons made a final search of the vessel. Hammett discovered the missing $20,000 under the scuppers on a lower boat deck. He had muffed his chance for a free trip—why couldn't he have been out to sea when he made the "discovery"? Furious with himself, he soon resigned as a Pinkerton operative.

(This incident illustrates an important facet of Hammett: he had operating throughout his life almost a religion of integrity. It's said if he ever gave his word, he always kept it. A good example of this is when in 1948 a doctor told Hammett he would die within six months if he did not stop drinking. Hammett began heavy drinking in the early 1920s, and drank destructively from 1930 until 1948. He told the doctor he would quit. The doctor, however, told Lillian Hellman in private that Hammett would not be able to quit, in his opinion, and that Hammett was close to finished. But Hammett *did* quit. A few years later Hellman mentioned to him what the doctor had said and Hammett was puzzled: hadn't he given the doctor his *word?* Hellman said, "Have you always kept your word?" Hammett answered, "Most of the time, maybe because I've so seldom given it.")

Also, from clues in the first Op novel *The Big Knockover,* it is apparent that the fictitious Continental Detective Agency (modeled directly on Pinkerton) had *its* offices in the James Flood Building as well. Therefore, if you walk through from the rear entrance on Ellis to the Market Street doors, you're treading the same marble that Hammett *and* the Op gumshoed over half a century ago.

Just next door to the Flood Building at 856 Market you will find:

The James Flood Building and the modern Samuels

27. Samuels Jewelers

After leaving Pinkerton Hammett hired in as an advertising writer for Albert Samuels Sr., and worked in the ad department until July, 1926. Of course, in the 1920s Samuels was located in the Lincoln Building at 895 Market—the southeast corner of Market and 5th Streets, half a block away and across the street from the store's present location. Samuels moved to the current site in 1943. Hammett dedicated his last Op novel, *The Dain Curse,* to Samuels, and based the character of Brigid O'Shaughnessy in part on Peggy O'Toole, a fellow employee in the ad department.

The famous Samuels street clock, a San Francisco landmark, stands before the store. It was installed on Market Street in February 1915 to coincide with the Panama-Pacific International Exposition, and it is the last stop on this tour.

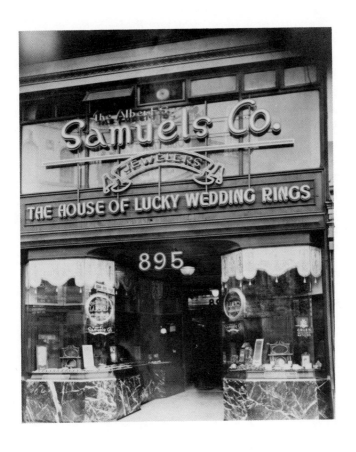

Samuels Jewelers, 1920s

Photo courtesy of San Francisco Archives, San Francisco Public Library

If you want more, you can look up the Pickwick Hotel at 5th and Mission, the last remnant of the name Pickwick Stage Terminal, where Sam Spade put the black bird in overnight storage. The actual bus terminal was in nearby Jessie Street. Less than half a block from the Pickwick is Remedial Loan at 932 Mission, the place Spade tells Brigid O'Shaughnessy will give her the best price for hocking her jewelry. You can hike up Telegraph Hill to Julius' Castle on Montgomery, where Spade and his secretary Effie Perrine eat lunch in the short story "A Man Called Spade." Or go up and down Spofford Alley and Waverly Place in Chinatown and soak up the atmosphere from the excellent Op story "Dead Yellow Women."

It is impossible to walk far in downtown San Francisco without crossing Hammett's trail.

BIBLIOGRAPHY

The following list is comprised of books or articles from which I have gleaned and collated information. Items of literary criticism, however interesting, are not included here; the enterprising Hammett fan will find the growing body of critical writing about Hammett's fiction detailed in Nolan's bibliographies.

Brady, Matthew: "Sam Spade City . . . just around the corner," *Hyatt on the Square* vol. 3, no. 1. A short article on Hammett sites within easy walking distance of the Hyatt Regency Hotel on Union Square, crediting Howard Gossage for his part in placing the plaque in Burritt alley.

Fechheimer, David: "Mrs. Hammett is Alive and Well in L.A." *City of San Francisco,* vol. 9, no. 17, Nov. 1975. An interview with Josephine Dolan Hammett, the single best source of information about Hammett's San Francisco years. Fechheimer, a partner in the famous Hal Lipset detective agency, was responsible for pulling this issue of *City* together.
————. "We Never Sleep" and "I Slept with Man O' War" also in *City,* Nov. 1975. Interviews Fechheimer conducted with ex-Pinkerton operatives Phil Haultrain and Jack Knight.

Gores, Joe: "A Foggy Night," *City,* Nov. 1975. An essay which pinpoints many Hammett locations which previously were in doubt, as well as presenting a case for actual buildings which Hammett may have used under other names in his stories. The most thorough survey of sites from Hammett's San Francisco stories to date.

————. "Author's Note," *Hammett,* G.P. Putnam's Sons, NY, 1975. Mentions sources used in this novel, some of which, however, are unreliable. Gores states, regarding Hammett's years in San Francisco, "the wife who shared some of them is dead;" later in that year David Fechheimer interviewed her.

Hammett, Dashiell: "Introduction," *The Maltese Falcon,* Modern Library, NY, 1934. Regarding the origins of the novel and the actual people he modeled his characters on.

Hammett, Richard T.: "Mystery Writer was Enigmatic Throughout Life," *Baltimore News-American,* Aug. 19, 1973. Hammett's nephew gives information on his family history.

Hellman, Lillian: *An Unfinished Woman,* Little, Brown, NY, 1969. Many anecdotes of Hammett from their almost thirty years together.

————. "Introduction," *The Big Knockover* by Dashiell Hammett, Random House, NY, 1966. A fine memoir of her relationship with Hammett; it

is used as the last chapter in *An Unfinished Woman.*
————. *Pentimento,* Little, Brown, NY, 1973. More
anecdotes concerning Hammett.
————. *Scoundrel Time,* Little, Brown, NY, 1976.
An account of her testimony before the House
Committee on Un-American Activities, with information on Hammett's trial and imprisonment
and the political atmosphere of the time. (Hellman's memoir volumes also contain photographs
of Hammett. Recently, the three books were
collected in one volume as *Three* by Lillian Hellman, Little, Brown, NY, 1979.)

Layman, Richard: *Dashiell Hammett: A Descriptive
Bibliography,* University of Pittsburgh Press, 1979.
The most complete listing of Hammett's work in
various media to date, with reproductions of
covers, *etc.*
————. *Shadow Man; The Life of Dashiell Hammett,*
Harcourt, Brace, Jovanovich, 1981. At this writing,
the most detailed biography of Hammett to appear.
Layman includes transcripts of Hammett's major
court appearances in the 1950s and several pages of
photographs.

Leiber, Fritz: "Stalking Sam Spade," *California
Living,* Jan. 13, 1974. The first walking tour
guide to *The Maltese Falcon.* A cornerstone
essay, now printed in the menu at John's Grill.

Nolan, William F.: *Dashiell Hammett: A Casebook,* McNally & Loftin, Santa Barbara, 1969. The first book-length survey of Hammett's life, Nolan's *Casebook* cannot be considered the equal of Layman's *Shadow Man* because it was written and published at a time when Hammett's papers were unavailable to scholars, and before David Fechheimer did his remarkable research on Hammett's San Francisco years. The *tone,* however, rings true. Nolan is working on a full-scale biography, incorporating all recently discovered information, to be titled *Life at the Edge.* The bibliography in this edition is still useful, and Nolan has updated it twice in the magazine *The Armchair Detective:* first in issue 4, vol. 6, 1973; more recently in issue 4, vol. 9, 1976.

Samuels, Albert S. Jr.: "A. Samuels tells the story of the famous Samuels street clock," *San Francisco Examiner,* June 3, 1980.

Tuska, Jon: *The Detective in Hollywood,* Doubleday, NY, 1978. A survey of detective films, with photos, including long sections on movies made from Hammett properties.

Yallop, David: *The Day the Laughter Stopped,* St. Martin's Press, NY, 1976. A book-length account of the Fatty Arbuckle trials.

Don Herron in the Hammett Room, John's Grill

about the author

Don Herron is a fan of Hammett and Raymond Chandler. In addition to the Dashiell Hammett Tour, he offers other walks covering sites associated with Robert Louis Stevenson, Ambrose Bierce, Ina Donna Coolbrith, George Sterling, Sir Arthur Conan Doyle, the Beats, Gertrude Atherton, Fritz Leiber, and numerous other authors who have lived or visited in San Francisco. His Literary Walking Tours have been striding up and down San Francisco's hills since 1977.

Herron co-edits the annual literary journal *The Romantist,* published out of Nashville, Tennessee. He has contributed essays on Stephen King, Jack Vance, Clark Ashton Smith, Dashiell Hammett, Russell Kirk, Robert E. Howard, and others to a variety of books and magazines. His first book, *Echoes from the Vaults of Yoh-Vombis,* is a biography of the late George F. Haas of Oakland, pioneer American mountain climber, occultist, and publisher of *The Bigfoot Bulletin.*

Herron has tried gumshoe work himself on rare occasions, working for a number of local agencies. He is a founder of The Maltese Falcon Society, an organization dedicated to Hammett and the hard-boiled school of detective fiction.